SEWING SHORTCUTS

TIPS, TRICKS & TECHNIQUES

SEWING SHORTCUTS
TIPS, TRICKS & TECHNIQUES

Pamela J. Hastings

Sterling Publishing Co., Inc.
New York

A Sterling/Sewing Information Resources Book

SEWING INFORMATION RESOURCES

Owner: JoAnn Pugh-Gannon
Photography: Kaz Ayukawa, K Graphics
Book Design and Electronic Page Layout: Ernie Shelton, Shelton Design Studios
Illustrations: Ernie Shelton
Index: Mary Helen Schiltz
Copy Editor: Mary Helen Schiltz

Library of Congress Cataloging-in-Publication Data

Hastings, Pamela J.
    Sewing shortcuts : tips, tricks & techniques / Pamela J. Hastings.
    p.   cm.
    "A Sterling/SIR book."
    "A Sterling/sewing information resources book"--T.p. verso.
    Includes index.
    ISBN 0-8069-0655-3
    1. Machine sewing. I. Title.
TT713.H358   1997
646.2--dc21   97-40616
                                                                          CIP

A Sterling/Sewing Information Resources Book

1 3 5 7 9 10 8 6 4 2

First paperback edition published in 1999 by
Sterling Publishing Company, Inc.
387 Park Avenue South, New York, N.Y. 10016
© 1998 by Pamela J. Hastings
Distributed in Canada by Sterling Publishing
c/o Canadian Manda Group, One Atlantic Avenue, Suite 105
Toronto, Ontario, Canada M6K 3E7
Distributed in Great Britain and Europe by Cassell PLC
Wellington House, 125 Strand, London WC2R 0BB, England
Distributed in Australia by Capricorn Link (Australia) Pty Ltd.
P.O. Box 6651, Baulkham Hills, Business Centre, NSW 2153, Australia
Manufactured in the China
All rights reserved

Sterling ISBN 0-8069-0655-3 Trade
              0-8069-7785-X Paper

About the Author

Pamela J. Hastings began sewing at the age of 12 making Christmas toys for the family pets. With the help of her high school home economics teacher, her sewing skills greatly improved and she moved on to more complex and creative projects!

After graduating from Keene State College in Keene, New Hampshire, with a degree in home economics, Pam began her career working for several companies in the home sewing industry. She has made numerous guest appearances on national and local television programs, hosted a sewing program on the Home and Garden Network as a spokesperson for the Singer Sewing Company as well as appeared in, wrote, and coordinated the Butterick "Sew by Video" series. She currently serves as spokesperson for several companies within the sewing industry.

Pam also is the author of the Sterling/Sewing Information Resources book, *Creative Sewing Projects with Computerized Machines.*

Pam resides in Wall, New Jersey, with her husband, Geof, and sons, Christopher and Connor.

Dedicationed To: Christopher Bruce (and Godzilla)

Acknowledgements

Special thanks all the sewing machine experts who took time out of their busy schedules to add their ideas, tips, and techniques to this book. They are:

Bernina of America—Susan Beck, Barbara Mix, Sara Meyer, Deborah May

Brother International Corporation—June Mellinger, Keri Morales

New Home Sewing Machine Company—Mary Carollo

Husqvarna Viking®—Nancy Jewell, Sue Hausmann, Nina Kay Donovan, Cathy Wilson

Baby Lock USA—Ann Heitkamp, Kelly Latreille

Pfaff American Sales Corporation—Laura Haynie, Chris Halik

Elna USA—Paula Spoon

Thanks to Ernie Shelton for the wonderful illustrations and to Kaz Ayukawa for the great photos. And once again, thanks JoAnn for your creative scheduling and talking me into doing a project I was hesitant to do and doing it in about half the time I thought I would need!

SEWING SHORTCUTS
TIPS, TRICKS & TECHNIQUES

Introduction

Shortly after I agreed to do this book, I had a major panic attack. What kind of techniques could I come up with that had not already been covered in one of the numerous technique books already available? Why did I agree to this?

I sat in my sewing room looking through all sorts of books, both old and new, as well as sewing publications and even pattern instruction sheets. As I looked through everything, I discovered techniques I had used once or twice that really worked and I loved. I also found techniques that I always meant to try.

After fine-tuning my favorite techniques, experts from the sewing machine companies were invited to share their favorite sewing methods and secrets. In addition to techniques to perfect clothing construction, we have included ideas for making better use of decorative stitches, tips for using presser feet, serger tricks, and techniques to inspire the decorator in you.

In the end, writing this book has been a pleasure—I've learned some new tricks and have been inspired to finally sew something new with all that fabric I have stashed away!

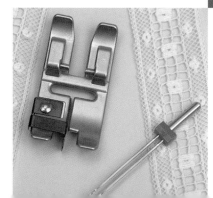

Chapter 1

A *home-sewn garment that looks as though it*

was purchased in the finest dress shop is the goal of

every sewer. The ideal fabric, a stylish pattern,

and a great fit, however, mean nothing if the fine

points of garment construction are overlooked.

Smartly sewn zippers and pockets, added details like

topstitching, and special care when sewing knits

will ensure that your sewing projects will leave

your friends wondering . . . did she or didn't she?

Zippers

Zippers are making a statement of their own in fashions today. Although the most common zipper is the centered zipper, lapped and invisible zippers are being used more and more frequently. Lapped zippers are best for the side seam of pants. Moving the zipper to the side reduces the bulk of a fly front and gives a garment a more slimming effect. Invisible zippers add a touch of sophistication and a true designer touch to any garment.

LAPPED ZIPPERS

1 Measure and mark the length of the zipper opening, using the zipper as a guide. Beginning at the edge of the seam, stitch with a regular machine stitch. Backstitch at marking and continue sewing the zipper opening with a basting stitch.

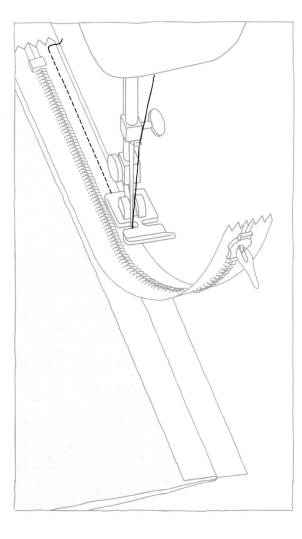

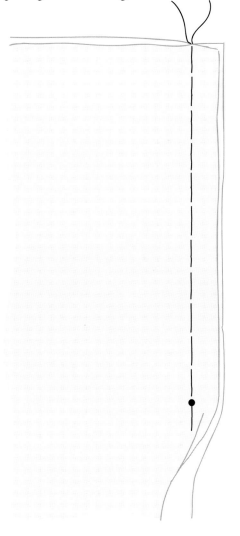

2 Press the seam open (side seams should be pressed over a pressing ham to keep their curved shape). Open the zipper and place it facedown on the right-hand seam allowance. The top of the zipper coil should be 1″ from the top edge of the garment. Pin, then machine-baste in place.

LAPPED ZIPPERS *continued*

3 Close the zipper and turn it faceup. Fold the seam allowance back so fabric is close to, but not covering, the zipper teeth. Beginning at the bottom of the zipper, stitch along folded edge through all thicknesses.

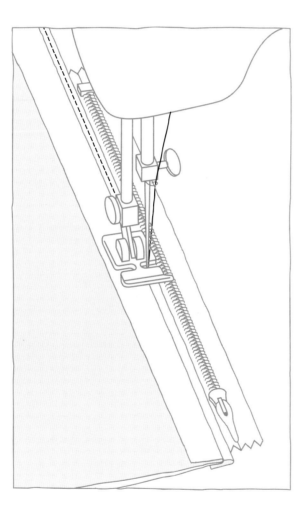

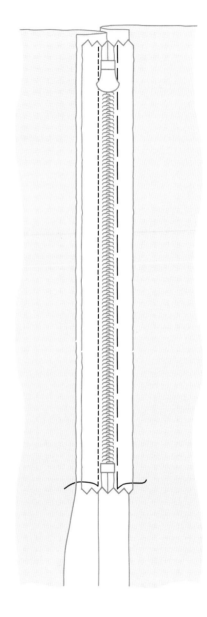

4 Spread the seam flat and place the remaining zipper tape on the remaining seam allowance. Make sure the pull tab is up. Beginning at the top of the zipper, machine-baste through the tape and the seam allowance.

5 Turn the garment to the right side and topstitch ½″ from the seam. Use a piece of ½″-wide tape as a stitching guide. Simply place the tape at the bottom of the zipper and along the seam. Begin stitching at the seam line at the base of the zipper, pivot, and continue sewing to the top of the garment edge.

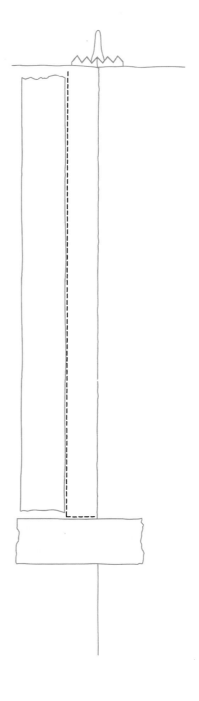

INVISIBLE ZIPPERS

Sue Hausmann, Husqvarna Viking®

To insert an invisible zipper, Husqvarna Viking® suggests using the buttonhole or "C" foot available with the Husqvarna sewing machines. This foot has two grooves on the underside just like the invisible zipper feet from years ago.

Always work with the zipper open and insert before sewing the final garment seam. Press the zipper flat, then place the left side of the zipper facedown on the left garment piece; the raw edge of the garment and the edge of the tape should be even.

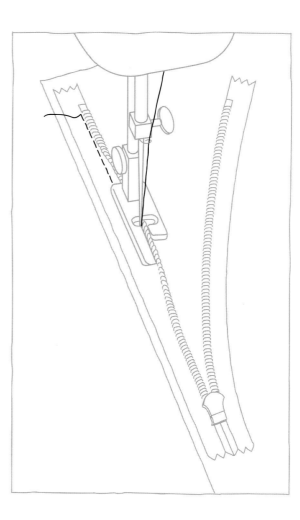

Invisible Zippers *continued*

2 Align the zipper teeth under the left groove of the foot. Adjust the needle position to stitch as close as possible to the zipper teeth. Stitch from the top of the zipper to the bottom. Repeat for the right side of the zipper, aligning the zipper teeth in the right groove.

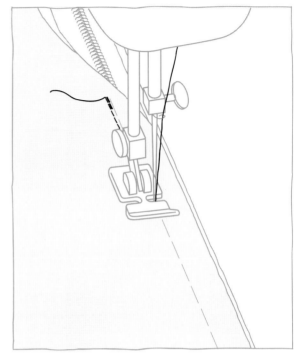

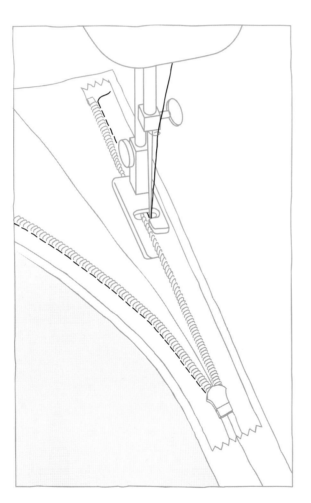

3 Close the zipper and replace the buttonhole foot with the zipper or "E" foot. Pin the remaining garment seam and stitch in place beginning a few stitches above the end of the zipper stitching.

Collars and Necklines

Although everyone is always looking for shortcuts, the following techniques are well worth the time and effort to make your garment look picture-perfect.

Hairline seams are ideal for sheer and lightweight fabrics and create nearly invisible seams.

Press and topstitch a collar that will look like it came right off the runway. The pressing technique was taught to me by my high school home economics teacher, Sara Reed. At the time, it seemed like a tedious exercise, but I still use it today. The topstitching technique is guaranteed to prevent bunching at collar points.

HAIRLINE SEAMS

I With right sides together, stitch a ⅝″ seam using a short stitch length. Stitch the seam a second time, using a narrow zigzag stitch next to the original line of stitching.

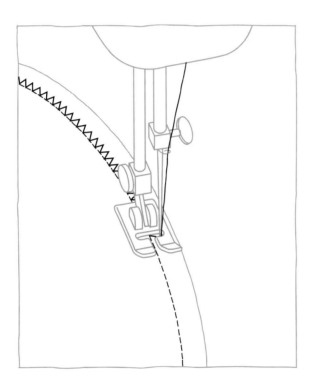

2 With small sharp scissors, trim the seam close to the zigzag stitch, taking care not to cut through the stitching. Turn right side out and press.

PRESSING COLLARS

1 Construct the collar according to the pattern directions, trim the seam, and turn the collar right side out.

2 Thread a hand-sewing needle with a contrasting thread. Insert the needle into the seam just under the stitching. Gently pull the stitching line "out" of the collar and hold it in place with your fingers. Remove the needle and take a basting stitch where the seam has been pulled out.

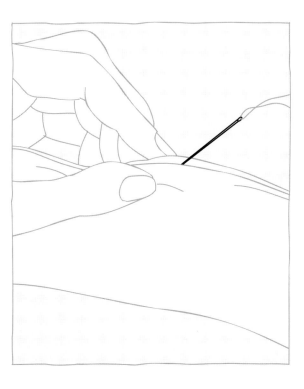

3 Continue this procedure around the entire collar. Press the collar using the point of the iron, so the basting stitches do not leave indentations in the fabric. Remove the basting—a beautifully pressed collar!

TOPSTITCHING POINTED COLLARS

1 Construct collar, turn, and press. By hand, sew one stitch in each collar corner and leave a long thread tail.

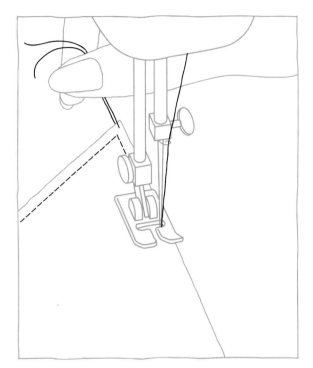

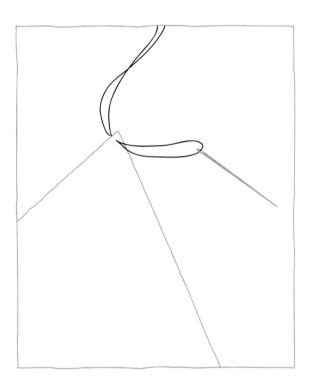

2 Beginning at the base of the collar, stitch to the point. With the needle down, raise the presser foot and turn the fabric, then lower the presser foot. Begin stitching again, holding on to the thread tails.

TOPSTITCHING ON NECK EDGES

Keri Morales, Brother International Corporation

Keri suggests using this technique to duplicate a European design trick. It really is a great look!

1 After sewing in the neck facing, trim the seam and press facing to the inside of the garment. Using a short stitch length, topstitch ¼″ away from the neck edge.

2 Stitch a second row of topstitching ¼″ away from the first row. Repeat until you have four or five rows of topstitching.

Knits

Knits are the ideal fabric for sewing with a serger and are, for the most part, simple to work with. There are, however, times when a conventional machine is required, and if you are sewing horizontally across the knit, it can mean stretching. Using the following techniques, buttonholes and hems can be done without ripples or headaches, and look just like ready-to-wear.

BUTTONHOLES

1 Mark the placement of the buttonholes on the garment front. Cut two strips of lightweight, tear-away or water-soluble stabilizer. Sandwich the buttonhole area between the strips of stabilizer.

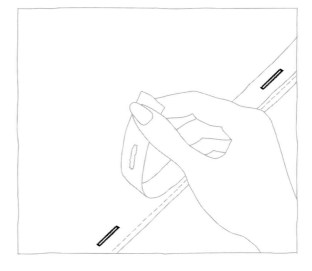

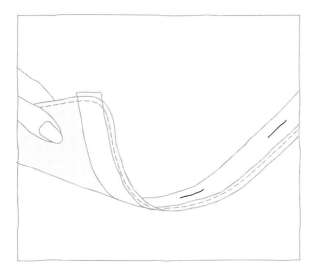

2 Stitch the buttonholes through all the layers. Gently remove the stabilizer from both sides of the garment. If using a water-soluble stabilizer, tear away the stabilizer, then rinse away the remaining residue.

HEMS

1 Measure the desired hem and turn up. Press the hem in place by lifting and placing the iron on the fabric.

2 Reduce the pressure on the presser foot (refer to your instruction manual for the proper procedure) or press lightly on the back of the presser foot while stitching to create built-in ease.

3 If there is still some fabric distortion, steam the hem back into place.

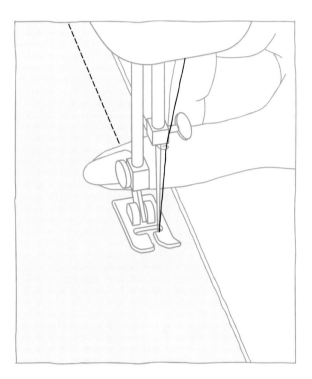

Unlined Patch Pockets

Patch pockets are basically easy to sew and can be added to almost any jacket or tailored shirt. The challenge is to create identical curves at the bottom edge. Follow these simple steps for using a pocket template and applying pockets for professional-looking results.

Unlined Patch Pockets *continued*

1 Complete the top edge of the pocket according to the pattern directions. Machine-baste along the sides and the bottom of the pocket just inside the seam line.

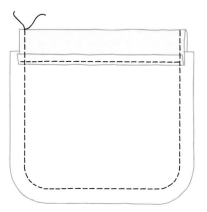

2 Cut a pocket template from cardboard using the finished pocket line on the pattern piece as a guide or use a two-piece metal pocket template set. Place the template down on the wrong side of the pocket and gather the machine-basting line around the edge of the template. (Add the second metal section if necessary.) Clip the corners or curves, and press. Remove the template. But *do not* press again.

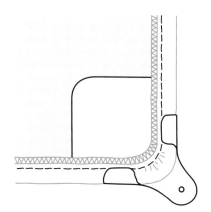

3 If possible, stitch the pocket to a flat garment piece before sewing the garment together. Baste the pocket in place using thin strips of fusible web. Edgestitch close to the folded edge.

Tip: For neater topstitching on your pockets, topstitch the pocket before basting the pocket in place. Then edgestitch as described above.

Elastic Insertion in Swimwear

Kelly Latreille, Baby Lock USA

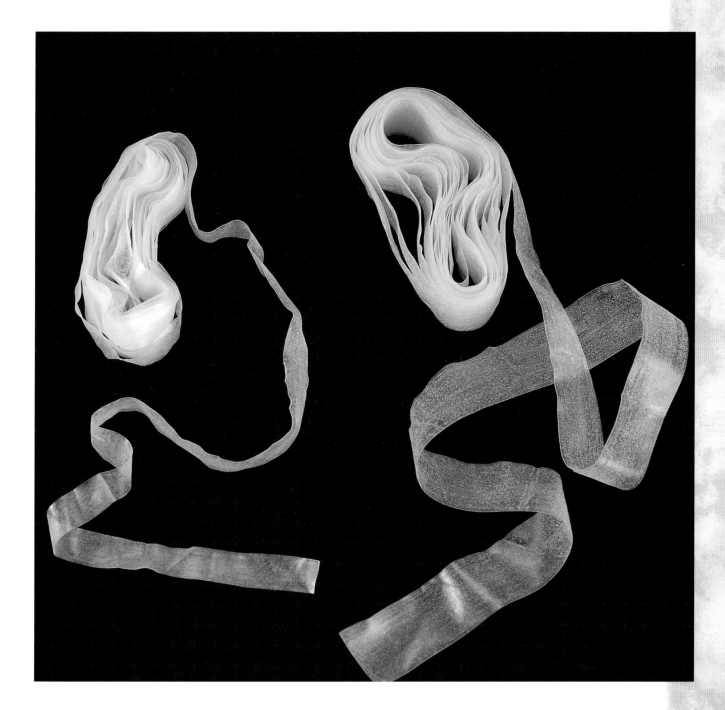

With the addition of the serger to the sewing room, making swimwear is easier than ever. For fuss-free elastic insertion, Baby Lock offers this technique using the elastic foot.

Elastic Insertion in Swimwear *continued*

1 Set your serger to a 3-thread overlock stitch, threading the loopers with Woolly Nylon® thread and the needle with all-purpose thread. If your machine has differential feed, set it to 0.6 and set the stitch length at 3mm–4mm.

2 Cut the elastic the length required by your pattern plus 1". Do not sew the ends of the elastic together.

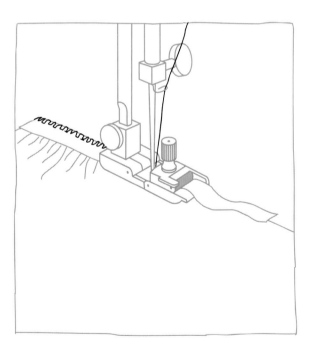

3 Insert the elastic into the elastic foot leaving a 1" tail in the back of the foot. Attach the foot to your serger. Change the stitch length to 4mm and begin stitching, tightening the screw on the foot while you are stitching in areas where the elastic needs to be stretched.

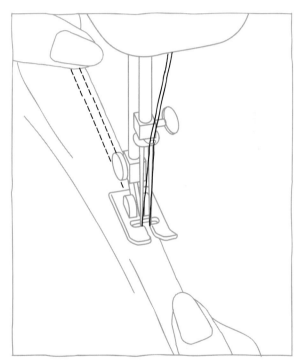

4 Turn under the elastic to the inside of the swimsuit. Using a long stitch length and a twin needle, topstitch the elastic in place on your sewing machine, stretching the elastic as you are sewing.

All-in-One Facings

Mary Carollo, New Home Sewing Machine Company

Basic techniques used in the garment industry can transform your garment from looking "homemade" to custom-made. Try this method of making neck and armhole facings for a beautifully finished garment. Rather than using the facing pieces included in your pattern, cut your own facing from the pattern pieces for the bodice front and back.

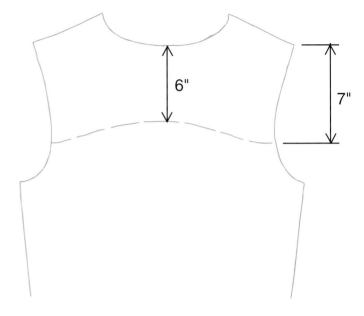

All-in-One Facings *continued*

1 For sleeveless garments, trace the upper portion of the garment front and back. Measure and place a mark 3″ down from each armhole and 6″ down from the center front or back. Draw a curved line connecting the marks to complete the new facing pattern.

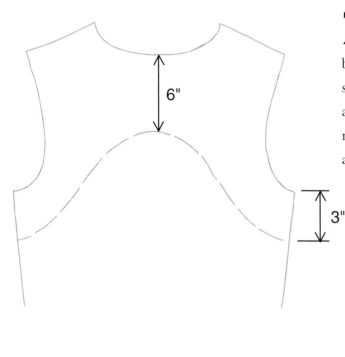

2 For garments with sleeves, again trace the upper portions of the garment front and back. Measure and mark 7″ down from each shoulder seam and 6″ down from center front and back. Draw a curved line to connect the marks. The extended facing will fall into the armhole seam and will always lay flat.

"Clip to the Dot"

Laura Haynie, Pfaff American Sales Corporation

Does "clip to the dot" make you tremble with fear? If so, you are not alone! Here's a wonderful technique that takes away the fear and the frayed clip marks. Clip-to-the-dot instructions are typically found with side seam pockets, collars, and front placket openings. Though the directions here are for a pocket, the same basic principle may be applied to the other areas.

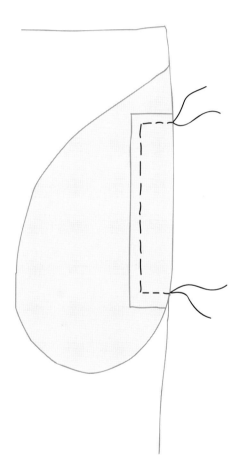

2 With right sides together, stitch the pocket to the garment front. Beginning at the side seams, stitch to the dot. Pivot and sew on the seam line to the next dot. Pivot and sew out to the side seam. Put Fray Check™ on the dots and clip to the dots. Turn the pocket to the inside and press. Attach the pocket to the garment back at the side seam.

I Interface the pocket area with a 1½"-wide strip of interfacing that begins and ends ½" above and below the dots on the wrong side of garment pieces.

"Clip to the Dot" *continued*

3 Place the garment front and back sections right sides together. Sew the side seam for the top down to the dot and backstitch. Fold the front pocket up and stitch from the dot to the bottom of the seam.

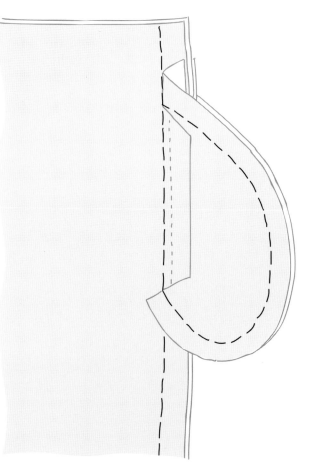

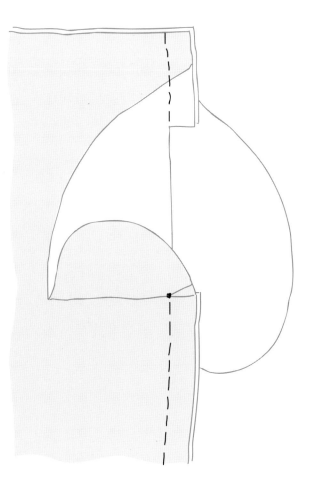

4 Trim the pocket side seam allowance to ¼". Understitch the pocket to the garment front. Complete by placing both pocket sections together and stitch around the edges from dot to dot.

Tips from the Experts

Use tricot knit interfacing to line any medium-to lightweight fabric that will be used for a jacket, vest, or pants. The interfacing helps to reduce wrinkles when traveling and gives the fabric more body.
Sara Meyer, Bernina of America

For a fit and style that's right for you, try on a ready-to-wear garment in a style similar to the pattern you are considering. This will help you decide if the garment is exactly what you want. Before you purchase your pattern, look at the measurements on the back of the pattern envelope. You will generally need a larger size than what you select in ready-to-wear. Don't be alarmed—pattern companies follow size guidelines that are different from companies in the garment industry.
Keri Morales, Brother International Corporation

To add new life to an old blazer, purchase new buttons and add a bit of interest with decorative stitching on the lapels or cuffs. Or add an embroidered crest to your jacket by simply opening the lining and placing the jacket in the embroidery hoop attached to the sewing/embroidery machine. You'll have a fresh new look in minutes!
June Mellinger, Brother International Corporation

Interface all the pocket openings even if the pattern does not call for it. Interface all kick pleats and walking slits. They will crease less and hang straighter. Better-quality ready-to-wear always has interfacing in these areas. Next time you go shopping—take a peak!
Laura Haynie, Pfaff American Sales Corporation

Chapter 2

There is an endless assortment of presser feet offered

by every sewing machine company. Presser feet have

been designed to make sewing more pleasurable and

make difficult tasks, like narrow hemming and applying

pearls, easier. Some feet, such as the tailortack foot

and some blindhem feet, can be used for a variety of

functions. Don't be afraid to play with different feet.

Sewing is much more fun when you get beyond the

straight-stitch foot, zipper foot, and buttonhole foot.

Narrow-Hem Foot

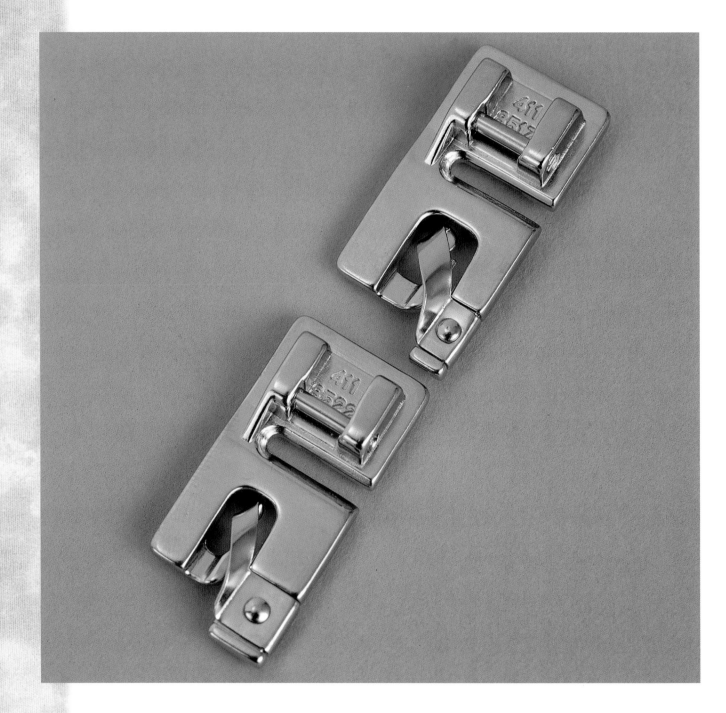

This foot creates perfect narrow hems on all types of fabric. The fabric scrolls through the foot to create a double-turned and stitched hem. Although it may be a bit tricky to use at first, after a few practice hems, you won't want to be without it.

1 To begin the scrolling process, fold under the first 1″ of the hem twice and press. Place the folded edge under the presser foot and sew a few stitches. Leaving the needle in the fabric, raise the presser foot.

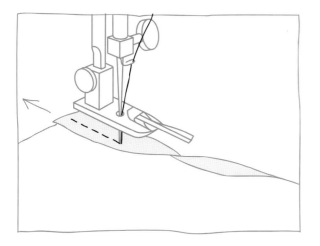 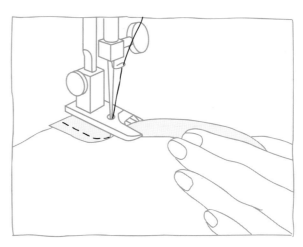

2 Guide the first fold into the scroll of the presser foot, being sure to hold the fabric taut. Lower the presser foot and begin sewing. Continue guiding the fabric by lifting it slightly so it feeds into the foot evenly.

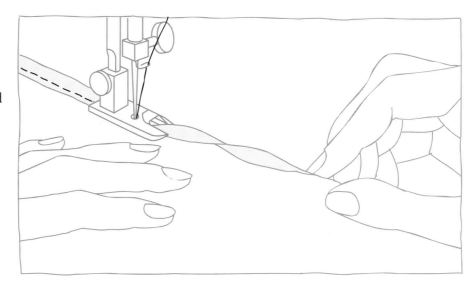

3 For perfect circular hems, begin sewing the hem as described above. Stop stitching about 1½″ from the starting point. Fold the remaining hem under; replace the hem foot with a straight-stitch foot and topstitch the remaining portion of the hem in place.

Decorative-Stitch or Embroidery Foot

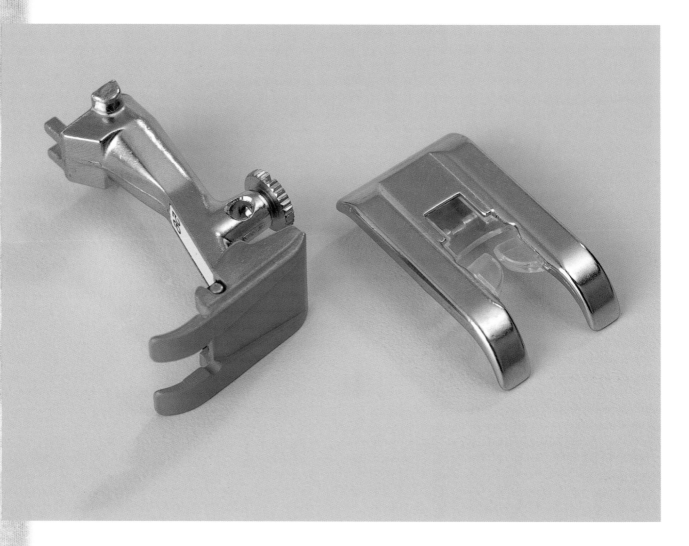

Most of today's sewing machines come with a decorative-stitch foot. This foot is either Teflon™-coated or has a large, fan-shaped or rectangular groove on the underside. This foot glides easily over raised satin and decorative stitching to prevent distortion, particularly when sewing extra-wide decorative stitches.

The Teflon version of this foot has a nonstick coating which also allows it to glide smoothly over sticky fabrics, such as vinyl and leather. Without the decorative-stitch foot, stitches can bunch up and become distorted. Perfect decorative stitches are the result of stabilizing the fabric and using the decorative-stitch foot.

Pearls-and-Piping Foot

June Mellinger, Brother International Corporation

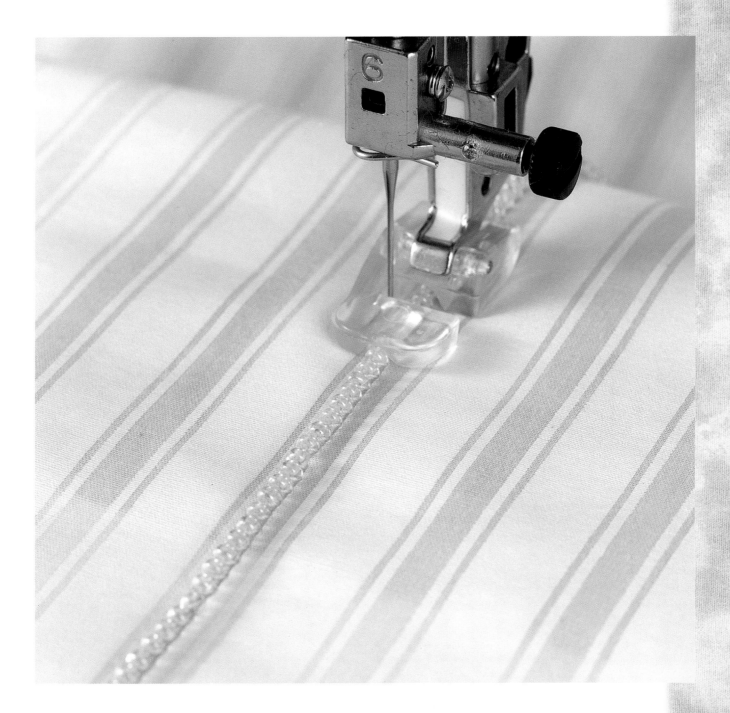

Embellishing garments and fabrics is more popular than ever, and the pearls-and-piping foot makes the job very easy.

Pearls-and-Piping Foot *continued*

3 Place the string of cross-locked pearls over the marked line and under the groove of the foot. Turn the handwheel to be sure the zigzag stitch clears the pearls. Begin sewing, guiding the pearls along the marked lines.

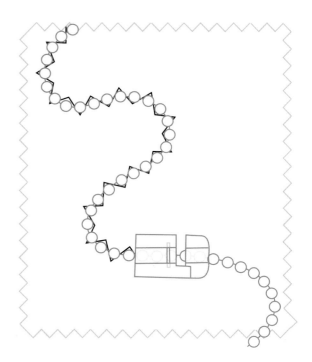

1 On the right side of your fabric, mark the desired design lines. Test the marking pen or chalk on a scrap of fabric to be sure it can be removed easily.

2 Place the pearls-and-piping foot on your sewing machine and thread the machine with transparent or monofilament thread. Set the stitch to a medium zigzag stitch.

Bias-Binder Foot

Paula Spoon, Elna USA

The bias-binder foot is a must-have for sewing coordinating bias binding onto any project. The extension on the front of the foot actually wraps the bias strip around the edge of the fabric as you are sewing.

Bias-Binder Foot *continued*

1 Cut 1″- wide bias strips from your fabric. Cut the ends diagonally for easy feeding into the foot. Pull the end of the strip toward the needle hole of the foot.

2 Insert the edge of the fabric into the side opening of the bias guide. Sew slowly, guiding the fabric edge with your left hand by placing your finger on the finger rest. With your right hand, guide the bias strip smoothly and evenly into the tape guide.

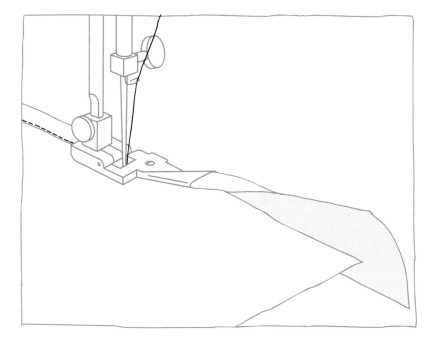

Tailor Tack Foot

Barbara Mix, Bernina of America

The tailor tack foot makes ⅝"- long fringe without a second thought. Fringe may be used as a decorative accent on craft projects and garments, or for practical purposes such as adding length to table linens or a child's dress. This foot also may be used to create extra-wide fagotting or for joining fabrics.

Tailor Tack Foot *continued*

1 Set the sewing machine for a zigzag stitch with a width of 2mm and a satin stitch length. Reduce the needle tension to 1. Attach the tailor tack foot to your machine.

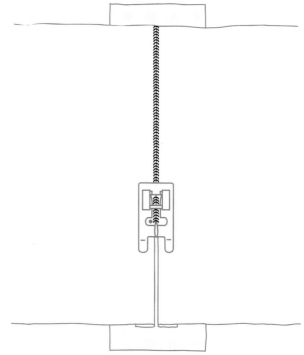

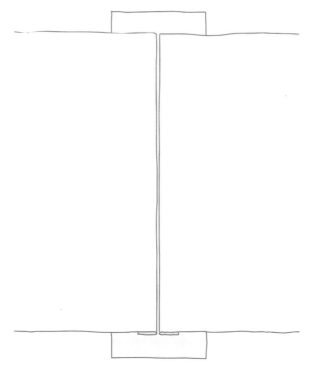

2 Turn under the seam allowance along the edge of two pieces of fabric and press in place. Using a stabilizer, butt the two folded edges together and center under the presser foot with right sides up.

3 Guide the fabric so the butted edges lie directly under the rise of the presser foot. Continue sewing, making sure that the left needle swing enters the left fabric and the right needle swing enters the right fabric.

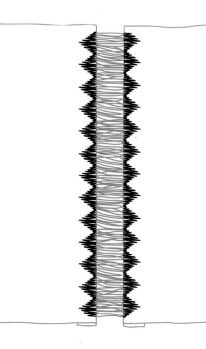

4 After stitching the length of the fabric, carefully remove the bobbin thread from the stitching and gently separate the two fabrics, leaving them joined by the upper thread.

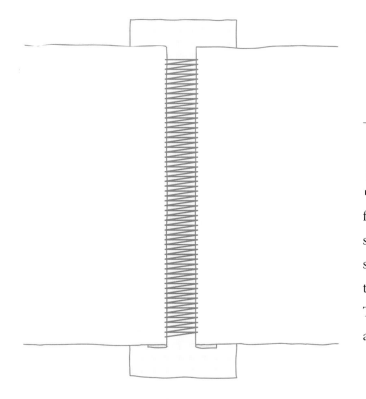

5 Select a flat-sided decorative stitch on your machine and replace the tailor tack foot with the embroidery foot. From the right side, anchor the fringe to the fabric by over-sewing the edge with the selected stitch. After the fringe is secure, gently remove the stabilizer. Trim away the excess seam allowance with appliqué scissors.

Narrow-Edge Foot with Twin Needles

Laura Haynie, Pfaff American Sales Corporation

Stitch lace to fabric quickly and easily using a twin needle and the narrow-edge foot.

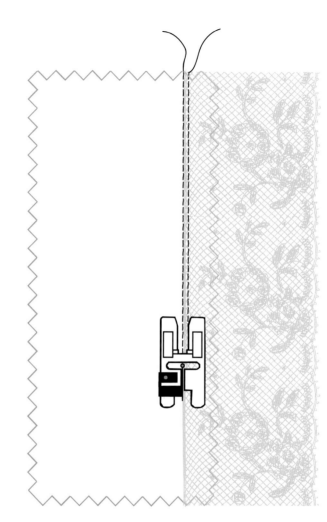

I Attach a size 1.6mm twin needle and the narrow-edge foot to your sewing machine. Thread the left needle with a color that matches your fabric and the right needle with a thread that matches your lace.

2 Sew with the fabric to the left and the lace to the right. Set the machine to dual feed to evenly feed both the lace and the fabric. Use Fray Check™ on the edge of the fabric after stitching. Let dry and trim the fabric close to the lace.

Dimensional Sewing

Mary Carollo, New Home Sewing Machine Company

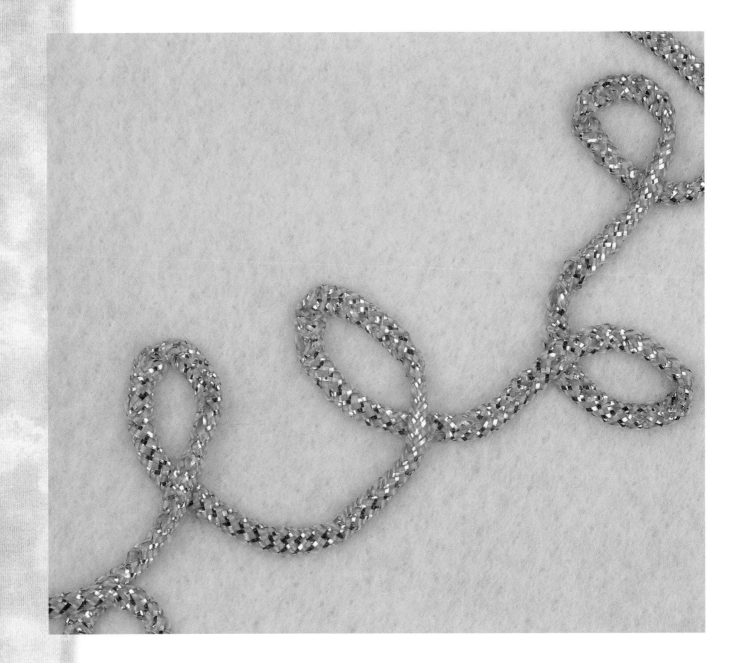

Thread painting over a printed design is a simple way to create an exquisite garment. Metallic or variegated thread can be used with a darning foot to fill in floral or geometric patterns. For a three-dimensional effect, you can outline with yarn, cord, or heavier decorative thread using New Home's Miracle Stitcher.

1 Back the fabric with stabilizer and set your machine to a straight stitch. Thread the machine with transparent thread or a thread that matches your decorative cord.

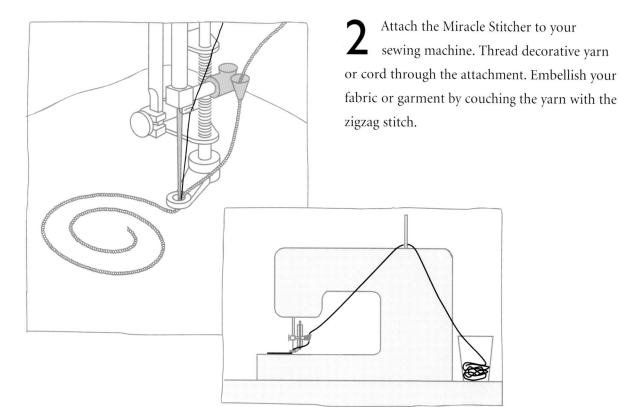

2 Attach the Miracle Stitcher to your sewing machine. Thread decorative yarn or cord through the attachment. Embellish your fabric or garment by couching the yarn with the zigzag stitch.

Tip: Use a small juice glass to hold the decorative cord. Place the glass next to the machine for consistent thread flow.

Blindhem Foot for Edgestitching and Topstitching

Kelly Latreille, Baby Lock USA

When topstitching extremely close to the edge on your cuffs, collars, lapels, and blouses, the blindhem foot and the positioning of the needle will produce superb results every time.

1 Attach the blindhem foot and set the sewing machine for a straight stitch in the left needle position.

2 Align the edge of your garment with the edge of the blindhem foot and lower the needle to check the positioning of the topstitching. Raise the needle and move to right or left as desired. Stitch close to the edge of your garment.

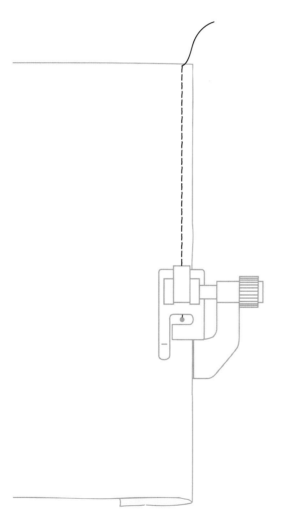

Tips from the Experts

For a delicate shell hem on tricot, use a rolled-hem foot and a vari-overlock stitch. Position the tricot into the scroll of the foot and set the length to 2.5mm and the width to 3.5mm.
Sara Meyer, Bernina of America

Bias-binder feet also can be used successfully when stitching in straight areas on a garment. Use strips of fabric that have been cut on the straight of grain rather than bias strips that will stretch and ripple in straight areas.
Laura Haynie, Pfaff American Sales Corporation

Chapter 3

It's no secret that all of us wonder what can be

done with the various stitches on our sewing machines.

The array of decorative stitches is tremendous on

today's machines, and they can be used to duplicate

Stitching Savvy

just about anything seen in ready-to-wear or home

furnishings. Blindhem stitches, the blanket-binding

stitch, and even the straight stitch can produce

impressive results with a bit of creativity.

Mock Hand-Picked Zipper

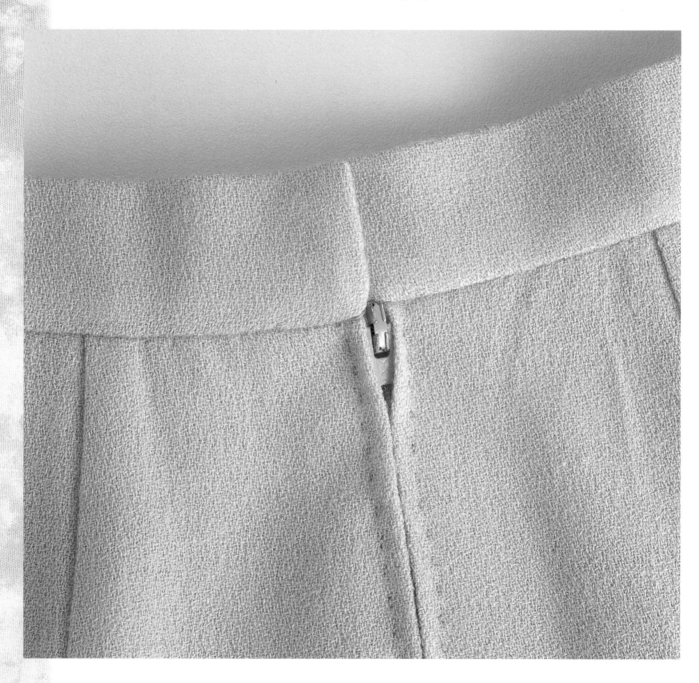

If you have always admired the couture look of hand-picked zippers, but were hesitant to tackle them, this is the technique for you. By using your blindhem stitch, you can insert a zipper with the look of hand-picking in a fraction of the time. Best of all, your stitches will look perfect every time.

1 You will need a zipper 1″– 2″ longer than the length required. Prepare your seam by sewing to the bottom of the zipper opening, back stitching, and machine-basting the zipper opening closed. Set the sewing machine for a blindhem stitch with a length of 2mm and width of 2.5mm.

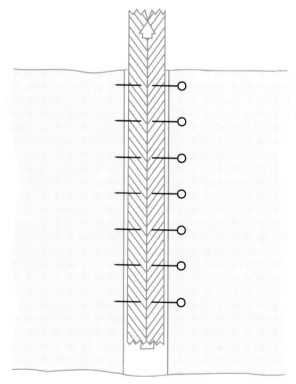

2 Close the zipper and position it facedown on the seam line. The base of the zipper teeth should be even with the bottom of the zipper opening, and the top of the zipper should extend beyond the garment edge. Pin the zipper in place with pins 1″ apart. Pins should be inserted so they enter and exit ¼″ on each side of the zipper tape.

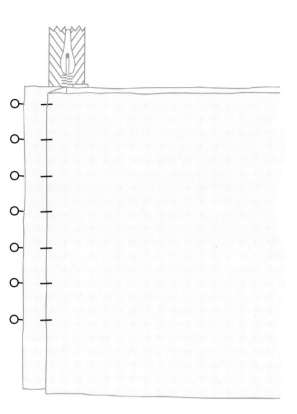

3 Place the garment piece with the zipper side down. Turn the fabric back to expose the seam allowance. Fold only as far as the point where the pins enter the fabric.

Mock Hand-Picked Zipper *continued*

4 Beginning at the base of the zipper, stitch along the seam allowance, removing the pins as you go. The zigzag of the blindhem stitch should enter the fold and the straight stitching should be positioned on the seam allowance.

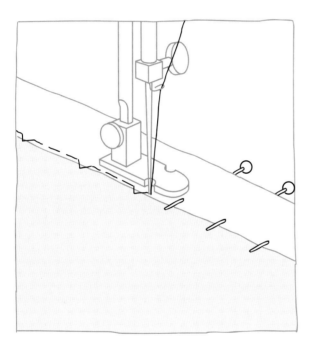

5 Repeat the procedure on the other side of the zipper. To ensure that the stitching is even, make a mark on the remaining seam allowance, indicating the location of the first zigzag of the completed side. The first zigzag of the remaining side should begin at this point.

6 Secure the bottom of the zipper tape by hand-stitching it to the seam allowances. Complete the garment according to the pattern directions. After applying the facings or waistband, bring the zipper pull down below the top edge of the garment and trim away any excess zipper tape.

Blanket-Binding Stitch

The blanket-binding stitch is one of the most versatile stitches on a sewing machine. Use it to create beautiful fringe and fagotting, as an elegant decorative detail, or as an alternative to the zigzag stitch for appliqué

FRINGE AND FAGGOTING
For a fringed edge:

1 For best results, use a plain-weave fabric with large fibers, such as linen. Cut the garment or project to the desired size or measurement. Determine the desired location and length of the fringe and measure from the raw edge for placement.

2 Beginning at one side of the fabric, pull out a weft (horizontal) thread the entire width of the fabric. This will be your stitching line. If a more visible line is needed, remove a second thread directly below the thread you just removed.

3 Set the machine to the blanket-binding stitch and sew a sample of the stitch to determine which direction the horizontal stitches fall. The horizontal stitches should fall to the left; use the mirror or reverse image to adjust if necessary.

4 Place the fabric under the presser foot right side up with the bulk of the fabric to the left. Insert the needle into the stitching line (line of pulled threads). Begin stitching with the vertical stitches in the stitching line and the horizontal stitches going to the left.

5 When the stitching is completed, simply fray the fabric below the stitching line.

FOR FAGGOTING

1 Determine the position of the desired faggoting on the garment. Mark the desired width of the fagotting and pull horizontal threads at each marking as described in the fringe instructions.

2 Stitching along the marked lines, the horizontal stitches of the blanket-binding stitch should face away from the center of the fagotting. After the stitching is completed, remove all the threads between the two lines of stitching.

APPLIQUÉ

1 Fuse or baste the appliqué piece to the sewing project. Set the machine to the blanket-binding stitch. Place tear-away stabilizer on wrong side of fabric.

2 Begin stitching around the edge of the appliqué. The vertical part of the stitch will fall directly on the edge of the appliqué and the horizontal part of the stitch should face the inside of the appliqué.

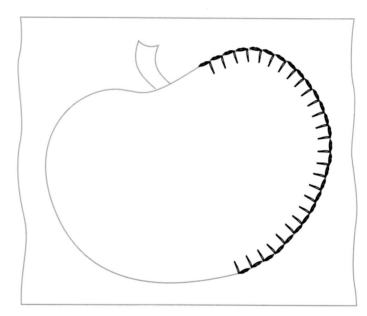

Reverse Bobbin Quilting

Paula Spoon, Elna USA

Use heavy decorative threads in the bobbin to create an interesting stitch that resembles rows of French knots. It's perfect for quilting fabrics or embellishing garments.

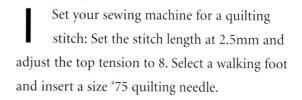

I Set your sewing machine for a quilting stitch: Set the stitch length at 2.5mm and adjust the top tension to 8. Select a walking foot and insert a size #75 quilting needle.

2 Thread the bobbin with a heavy decorative thread such as Ribbon Floss™, Pearl Crown Rayon™, or Madeira's Decor 6™. Mark the stitching lines on the wrong side of your quilt or garment. With the right side down, stitch along the marked lines.

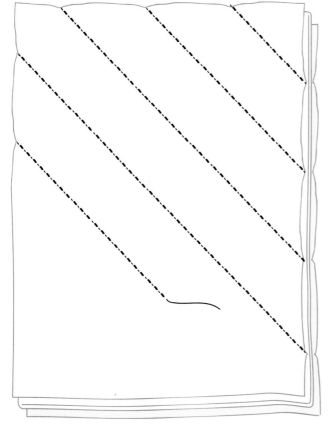

Easy Embroidered Sachet

Kelly Latreille, Baby Lock USA

Create beautiful one-of-a-kind sachets using the embroidery motifs on your computerized embroidery machine.

1 You will need: three 9″ x 9″ pieces of fabric, stabilizer, embroidery hoop, computerized embroidery machine, and the Esante embroidery card #9 or other appropriate design.

2 Mark the center of one square with chalk or a water-soluble marker. Place the stabilizer under the fabric and insert both layers into an embroidery hoop.

3 Select the flower motif #41 and press "LAYOUT" twice. Center the needle over the center mark on the fabric and begin sewing. When the embroidery is complete, remove the fabric from the hoop and mark the center point with two crossed pins.

Easy Embroidered Sachet *continued*

4 Fold the remaining fabric squares in half, wrong sides together, and press. Place the fabrics side by side, overlapping the folded edges by ½″, and pin.

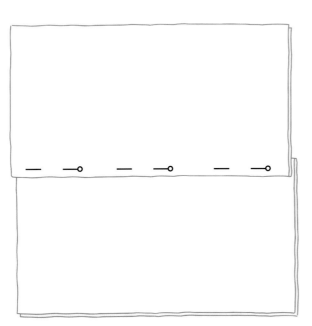

6 Remove the fabric from the hoop and apply seam sealant to the edges of the scallop stitch. When dry, carefully trim close to the stitching. Insert a small bag of potpourri or a cotton ball with a drop of oil or perfume through the opening in the back.

5 Place the embroidered square over the folded fabrics matching the outer edges. Place all of the layers into the embroidery hoop. Remove pins. Select the scallop frame motif #24 and embroider.

Filigree Lacemaking by Machine

Cathy Wilson, Husqvarna Viking®

Add a beautiful decorative touch to pockets and collars by adding filigree lace created on your sewing machine. This technique utilizes a variety of decorative stitches and works beautifully on linens for an heirloom accent.

Filigree Lacemaking by Machine *continued*

1 You will need: one 8″x10″ piece of cotton or linen for pocket, 3″x10″ strips of Heat-Away™ stabilizer, heavy topstitching thread such as Zwicky™ silk flora, and a topstitching needle.

2 Serge or overcast one 10″ edge of the pocket. Turn the edge to the wrong side and press. Attach an open-toe embroidery foot and insert the topstitching needle. Thread the machine and bobbin with the topstitching thread.

3 Place a strip of Heat-Away stabilizer under the finished edge of the pocket with the stabilizer extending at least 2″ beyond the edges.

4 Set the machine to one of the following stitches: a three-step zigzag (L–1.1mm, W–6mm); an arched scallop, mirrored side-to-side; a casing stitch (L–1.1mm, W–6mm); an heirloom appliqué stitch (L–3mm, W–4.5mm); or a large, side-motion double cross-stitch. (*Note:* These stitches are recommended for Viking owners; you may use a similar stitch on another sewing machine).

5 Stitch along the finished edge of the pocket so the far left swing of the needle catches the fabric edge and the remainder of the stitch is formed on the stabilizer.

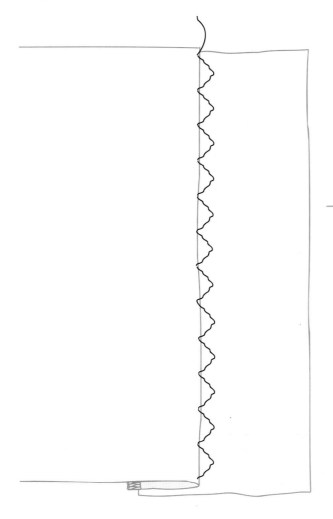

6 Stitch a second row of stitching. This time the left swing of the needle should just catch the thread of the widest part of the previous row. Stitch additional rows in this manner, as desired.

7 Trim away any excess stabilizer. To remove the remaining stabilizer from stitching, press from the wrong side with a DRY iron on the cotton setting until the stabilizer turns to a dark ash. Brush the ash away with a toothbrush. (Do not use steam as the moisture will keep the stabilizer from disintegrating and may damage the fabric.)

Quick-Tack Quilting

Mary Carollo, New Home Sewing Machine Company

Quick-tack quilting is the easiest method of keeping batting secured in a quilt. When this technique is done on your sewing machine, the process is even quicker. Single-pattern stitches are just perfect for this technique.

1 Layer your quilt top, batting, and backing in this order, then safety-pin all the layers together. Mark the fabric with the locations you will sew your tacking stitch.

2 Program your machine for a single-pattern stitch, such as a diamond or star. Beginning in the center of the quilt and working towards the outer edges, stitch the selected design on each placement mark.

Tips from the Experts

Rayon thread comes in various weights – the lower the number, the thicker the thread. Use #30 weight Sulky™ rayon thread for bolder-looking decorative stitches, rather than #40 weight embroidery rayon.
Sara Meyer, Bernina of America

For topstitching with a truly hand-stitched look, use Cotty 12™ thread. Available in a wide range of colors, Cotty 12 is a 100% cotton decorative thread.
Luny 12™ is a yarn-like embroidery thread. Use Luny 12 with embroidery designs that have been enlarged to the maximum. Luny 12 will fill in beautifully and give your embroideries the look of crewel embroidery.
Laura Haynie, Pfaff American Sales Corporation

Chapter 4

Sewing for the home can seem a bit daunting at first

because of the tremendous amount of fabric needed

for projects. But don't shy away from decorating. With

careful measuring and a few straight seams, you can

transform any room into a showplace. Working with

Decorating Details

stripes, matching fabrics, making perfect pillows,

and mitering trims are just a few techniques that will

make your decorative accessories look like they came

from a prefessional workroom.

Working with Stripes

With a bit of innovative cutting, an ordinary vertical or horizontal stripe can change dramatically. By simply changing the direction of the pattern pieces, you can create a variety of mitered effects that are great for pillows and tablecloths.

MAKING PATTERNS

1 For pillows and square tablecloths, draw a pattern 1″ larger than the desired pillow or tablecloth size. Divide the pattern into triangles. Trace the triangles onto Pattern-Ease™ or tissue paper, adding a ½″ seam allowance to the edges of the triangle. Make three additional pattern pieces to complete the square. Mark a grainline parallel to the outer edge of the finished square.

2 For circular tablecloths, create a square from brown paper that measures twice the drop length of the tablecloth plus the diameter of the table plus 1″. Fold the square into fourths. Tie a piece of string to a marking pen (the string should measure one half the finished diameter of the tablecloth). Hold the string at the folded corner of the square, pull the string taut, and draw an arc along the square. Cut on marked line.

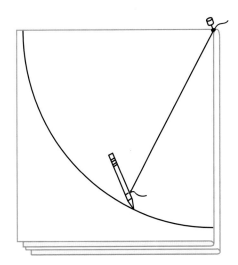

Making Patterns *continued*

3 Unfold the circle and place it on a flat surface. Trace one wedge of the circle onto tracing or tissue paper and add a ½″ seam allowance. To determine the grainline, fold the wedge in half, bringing the straight edges together; unfold and use the folded line as the grainline. Make three additional pattern pieces.

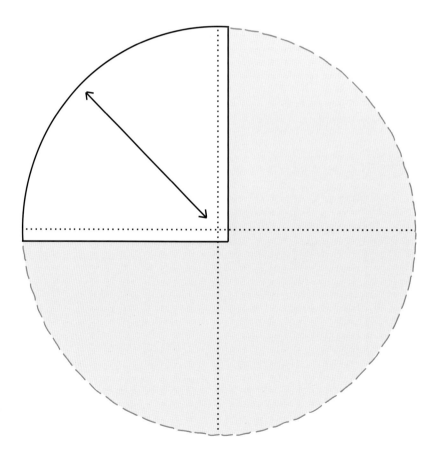

PATTERN LAYOUT

For a "square effect," place the pattern pieces so the grainline runs in the same direction as the stripes. Center the pattern pieces over the desired stripe. *Note*: Each pattern piece must be cut identically.

For an "X" design, place the pattern pieces so the grainline is perpendicular to the stripes, centering the pattern over the desired stripe. Again, each piece must be identical.

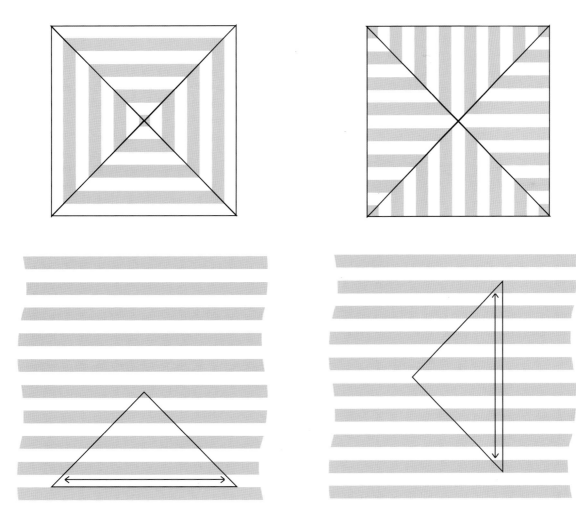

To assemble either design, simply stitch the triangle together with a ½" seam allowance.

Matching Fabrics

To effortlessly and flawlessly match printed home decorating fabrics, try this technique taught to me by Nancy Jewell of Husqvarna Viking®. After trying it once, I was so pleased with the results, I now use it all the time.

Matching Fabrics *continued*

I Finger-press a ½″ seam allowance along the edge of one fabric length. With right sides facing up, lap the pressed edge over the length to be matched. Match the prints and pin in place.

2 Set your sewing machine to a zigzag stitch (L–5mm, W–4mm). Using a blindhem or edgestitching foot, stitch along the fold on the right side of the fabric, removing pins as you sew. One swing of the zigzag should just pierce the fold; the other will go into the fabric. For best results, use a high contrast thread.

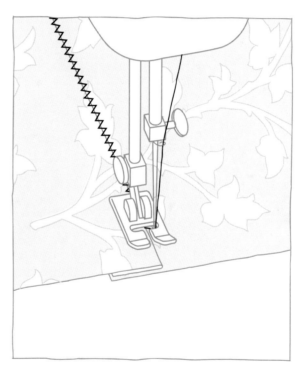

3 Unfold the fabric; the lengths of fabric will now be right sides together. You will see a "ladder" formed by the zigzag stitching. Rethread the machine with matching thread, select a straight stitch, and sew the fabric together with a ½″ seam. Remove the zigzag stitching.

Mitered Bands for Window Panels

Give a simple window panel a custom touch by adding contrasting bands. The bands may be as wide or as narrow as you wish and in any fabric compatible with your window panels. Try teaming a stripe or floral with a small allover print for a country cottage look, or use two contrasting solids for a more contemporary feel.

Bands generally are found on the leading (inside) edge and the bottom of curtain panels; however, contrasting bands are also appropriate along three sides of your curtain panel.

1 Cut your curtain panels to the desired sizes using measurements for the finished width by the finished length plus the heading. Piece the fabric as needed. If you are lining the panels, cut the lining to the same size and baste the fabric and lining, wrong sides together, along all sides.

2 Cut the border bands as follows: For the sides, cut two strips of fabric, the cut length of the curtain panel plus 1¼″ by twice the desired border width plus 1¼″. For example, if your finished border band is 1″ wide, the fabric strips should be 3¼″ wide. For the bottom edge, cut a strip of fabric the finished width of the curtain plus 1¼″ by the band width plus 1¼″.

3 Press each of the side bands in half lengthwise with wrong sides together. At one end (this will now be the lower corner), diagonally fold back the short edge to meet the fold; press. Unfold and cut along the diagonal folds. Repeat with the lower band, pressing and cutting diagonally at both ends of the band.

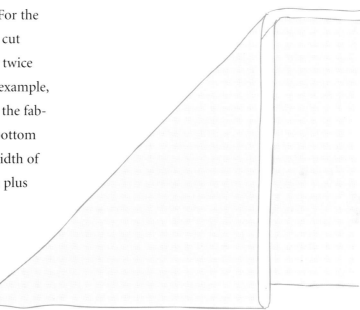

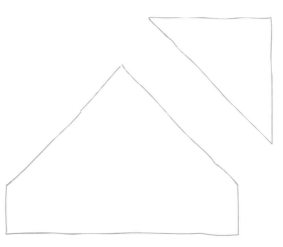

5 On the curtain bottom and sides, mark a placement line the width of the finished border minus ½″ from each raw edge. For example, if the finished border is 4″, mark a line 3½″ from the raw edge.

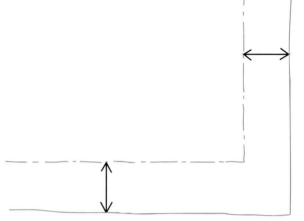

Mitered Bands for Window Panels *continued*

4 Place the lower and side bands with right sides together along the diagonal edges and pin. Stitch with a ½″ seam allowance beginning and ending ½″ from each side edge. Trim the tip of the seam. Open the band out flat and press open the lower seam allowance.

6 Pin the band to the lower edge of the curtain panel along the placement line. The seam of the band will be on the corner of the placement lines. Stitch the band in place, beginning and ending exactly on the mitered seam.

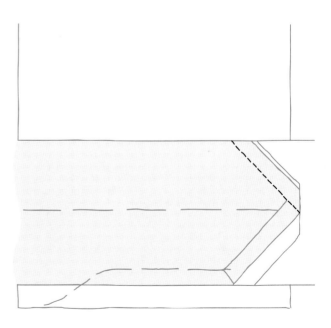

8 Turn the bands to the lining or wrong side of the curtain panel. Turn under ½" on the raw edge of the band and pin in place along the stitching line. Slipstitch in place. Finish the top edge of the panel as desired.

7 To attach the side bands, turn each band up along the side placement lines and pin in place. Open and press the outside mitered seam. Stitch the band in place, beginning or ending exactly on the mitered seam.

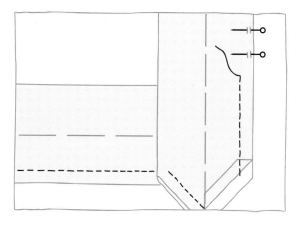

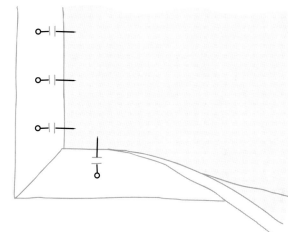

Rosettes

Use rosettes to add a decorative accent to tiebacks and table toppers, and as the finishing touch for pillows or the corners of swags. For best results, use a fabric with some body so the rosettes will hold their shape and not look limp.

1 Cut a circle of fabric about 25″ in diameter (may be made larger or smaller, if desired). Thread a hand-sewing needle with a strong, double thread and hand-gather along the outer edge of the rosette.

2 Pull up the stitches to tightly gather, tie the thread ends to secure, and clip the excess threads. Pull the gathered center out and wrap a rubber band one-third of the way down the opposite end of the rosette.

3 Flatten out the rosette, matching the gathers and rubber band (gathers should be on the bottom). Tack the center of the rosette to the gathers on the underside using small stitches. Pouf out the edges of the rosette.

Continuous Bias Strip

Bias strips are often used in home decorating for decorative edging or to make custom piping. Rather than cutting endless bias strips and piecing them together to create the required yardage, try this method for making continuous bias strips.

1 Cut a square of fabric and draw a diagonal line from corner to corner, forming two triangles. Cut along the marked line and mark each edge with a letter (A to F).

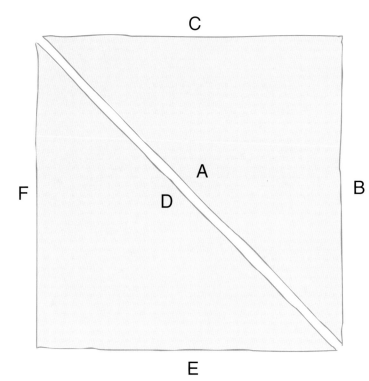

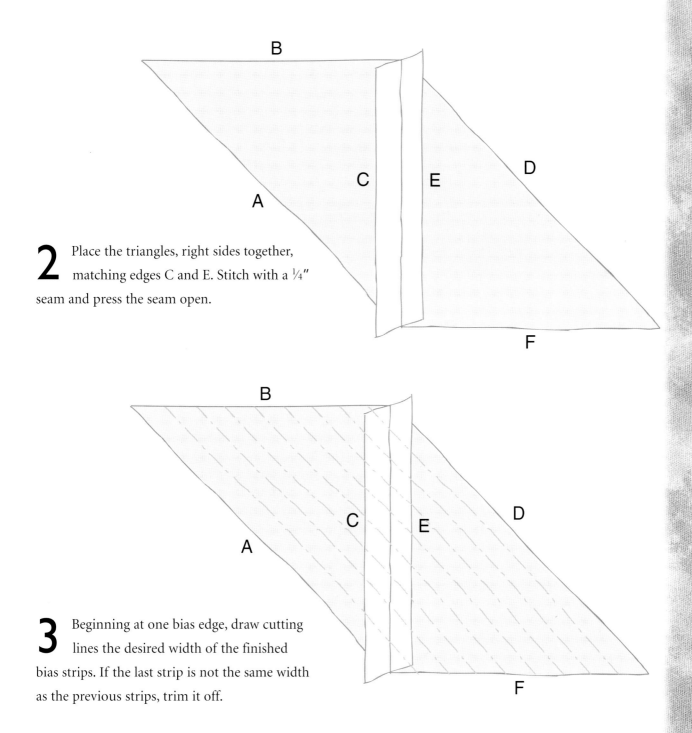

2 Place the triangles, right sides together, matching edges C and E. Stitch with a ¼″ seam and press the seam open.

3 Beginning at one bias edge, draw cutting lines the desired width of the finished bias strips. If the last strip is not the same width as the previous strips, trim it off.

Continuous Bias Strip *continued*

4 Fold the edges B and F, right sides together, and shift the cutting lines by one width so the bottom and top edges match up with the first and last marked lines.

5 Stitch with a ¼″ seam allowance and press the seam open. To cut a continuous strip, begin at one end of the fabric tube and cut along the marked lines.

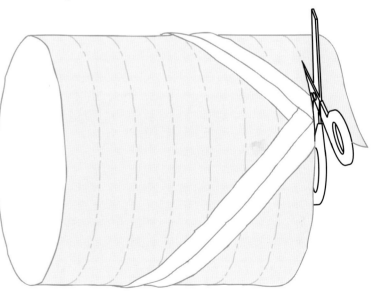

Piping and Cording

Piping (or cording) commonly is used for added interest on the edges of pillows, shams, and duvet covers. Piping is simply a filler cord that has been covered with fabric. It may be purchased or made from the decorator fabric you are working with. Filler cord is available in a variety of sizes and can be used to create a variety of looks.

PERFECTLY INSERTED PIPING

Follow these simple steps to add piping easily and perfectly. Although we have given directions for piping pillows, the same method may be used for any decorating project.

1 Pin the piping to the right side of one pillow front, with the raw edge of the piping even with the raw edge of the pillow. Clip the piping at the pillow corners to ease in place. Using a zipper foot, machine-baste the piping in place, beginning stitching 1″ from the end of the piping.

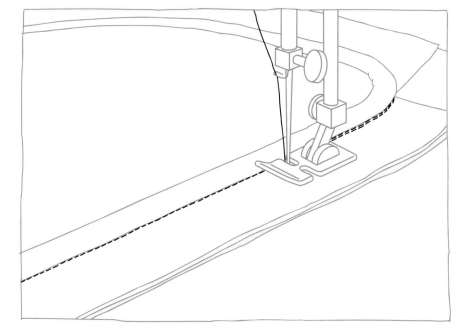

2 Stop stitching 2″–3″ from the starting point. Cut the piping so it overlaps at the starting point by 1½″. Remove the stitching from the cut end of the piping and open. Trim.

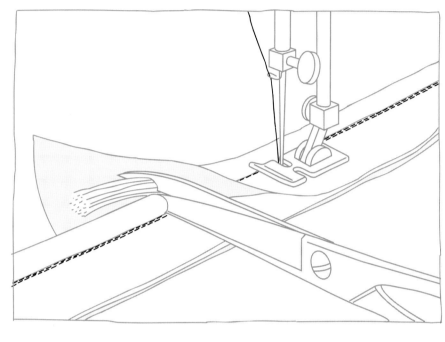

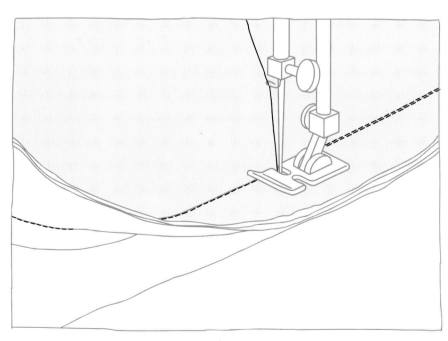

3 Place the pillow front and back, right sides together. Stitch with the piping piece up. Using the basting line as a guide, stitch the seam so the stitches fall between the piping and the basting stitches.

Attaching Jumbo Piping

Deborah May, Bernina of America

Piping, filled with a large filler cord, can be made quickly and easily with Bernina's leather roller foot. Smooth or shirred, it will add a decorative touch to edges and seams. Jumbo piping is ideal for home decorating projects, such as pillows, tablecloths, tiebacks, and headboards. Use smooth piping for a tailored look or shirred piping for a soft romantic feel.

1 Attach the leather roller foot and set the sewing machine for a straight stitch (L–2 to 4). Position the needle to the far left and set the needle stop to down.

2 To cover ⅝"- to 1"-wide filler cord, cut a bias strip of decorator fabric 3½" wide by the length of the piping piece needed. Thread the machine with nylon monofilament thread in the bobbin and needle.

3 Wrap the fabric, wrong sides together, around the filler cord. With the cord to the right of the roller foot, machine-stitch close to the cord.

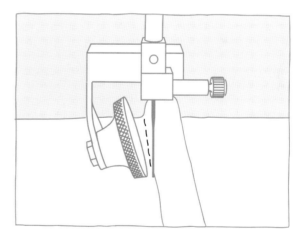

Attaching Jumbo Piping *continued*

4 For shirred piping: To cover ⅝″ to 1″ cord, cut the bias strips of fabric 4″ wide by twice the length of piping needed. Thread the needle and bobbin with monofilament thread.

5 Wrap the bias strip around the cord with wrong sides together. Stitch across the end of the cord, securing the cord to the fabric.

6 With the cord to the right of the roller foot, begin stitching close to the cord. Stop every 10″ - 12″ and pull the cord towards you. The fabric behind the foot will shirr.

7 To attach either type of piping, machine-baste the piping to the pillow with the raw edges of the piping even with the raw edges of the pillow top (the lip of the piping should be to the left of the presser foot and the bulk of your fabric to the right). You may have to roll up the pillow fabric so it will feed smoothly through the sewing machine. Complete your pillow as desired.

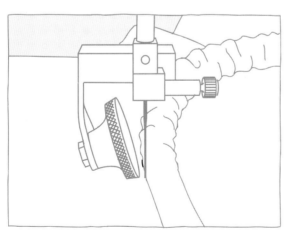

Serger Cover-Stitch Zipper

Sara Meyer, Bernina of America

Use the cover stitch on a serger for inserting zippers in the backs of pillows and other home decorating items. Because the cover-stitch foot is made to ride along different levels of fabric at the same time, stitching close to a zipper can be accomplished with ease. A cover-stitch zipper can be exposed or lapped.

1 Set the serger to the cover stitch. Using a zipper that is at least 4″ longer than your seam, open the zipper and stitch the zipper tape to each side of the pillow, right sides together.

2 Close the zipper, fold the fabric back, and press in place. For an exposed zipper, press the fabric back so the teeth are exposed. For a lapped zipper, fold the fabric back and butt the folds together. On the right side of your fabric, topstitch each side of the zipper in place using the cover stitch.

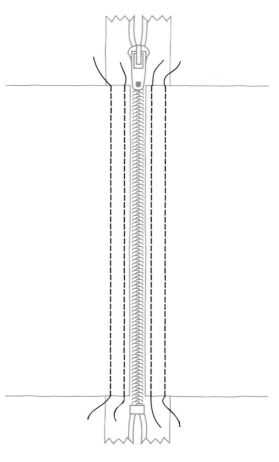

3 After sewing crossing seams, trim the excess zipper. (*Note*: Be sure to lower the zipper pull, before trimming away the top of the zipper tape.)

Simple Window Panels

Mary Carollo, New Home Sewing Machine Company

Changing the look and mood of a room is as easy as changing the window treatment. This simple treatment attaches the valance to the curtain panel so only one curtain rod is necessary.

1 For the curtain: Cut the fabric the desired finished length of the curtain plus 5″. Hem the curtain with a double-fold 2″ hem using a blindhem stitch or straight stitch.

2 For the valance: Cut the fabric the desired finished valance length plus 4″. Hem the valance with a double-fold 1½″ hem using the same stitch as above.

3 Hem the side of the curtain and valance with a double-fold 1″ hem. Stitch the hem using the previously selected stitch.

Press the seam open. Fold the valance
over the right side of the curtain panel,
osing the seam. To form a casing, stitch
' down from the top edge through all the
rs. (*Note*: Stitch a wider casing for wider
tain rods.)

Perfect Pillows

Nancy Jewell, Husqvarna Viking®

What's the difference between a square pillow you've purchased and one designed by you? The telltale difference is your pillow squares aren't square at all. They're nipped at the corners so when the fabrics are seamed and stuffed, they appear square, but prevent limp and empty corners like the pillows you've purchased.

1 To make a pillow, cut two squares of decorator fabric the finished size of your pillow plus 1″. With a fabric marker, mark a dot ½″ inside each corner of the pillow front.

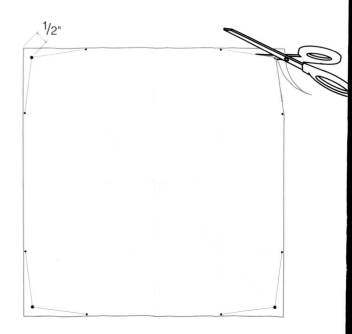

2 Fold the fabric in half, then fold the top layer back so the raw edge meets the fold. Make two dots—one on the center fold and one right next to it on the fabric. Fold the fabric in the opposite direction and repeat the process.

3 Connect the corner and the edge dots on all sides of the pillow. Trim along the marked line. Repeat the procedure with the pillow back or use the pillow front as a pattern for the pillow back. Sew the pillow together. The result—pillows that look perfectly square.

One-Step Serger Ruffles

Kelly Latreille, Baby Lock USA

Use the ruffling foot on your serger to create beautiful ruffled curtains. In one easy process, ruffles are finished and stitched to the flat fabric simultaneously.

1 Attach the ruffling foot to your serger. Place the fabric right side up under the presser foot. Place the flat fabric between the guides in the front of the foot, right side down.

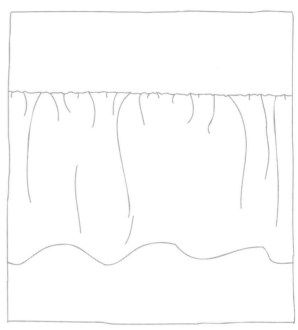

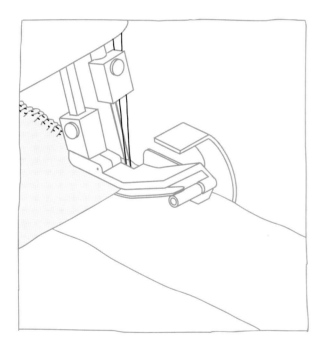

2 Pull the fabric toward the needle and place the edge of the fabric just inside the edge of the guide. Begin stitching, guiding the lower fabric with your right hand and the upper fabric with your left hand.

Trapunto Envelope Pillow

Chris Halik, Pfaff American Sales Corporation

Pillows are the easiest and least expensive way to add decorative accents to a room. For a sophisticated touch to a simple floral pillow, add trapunto to accent the motifs.

Tips from the Experts

1 Cut a floral decorator fabric to the desired finished size of the pillow plus 1″. Be sure to center a dominant floral motif before cutting. Cut a piece of muslin the same size as the pillow section.

2 Thread the sewing machine with monofilament thread in the needle and all-purpose thread in the bobbin. Place the muslin and decorator fabric wrong sides together. With the decorator fabric on top, stitch around the floral motifs.

3 Cut a small slit in the back of the stitched areas and add fiberfill through each slit, stuffing the area. Fuse paper-backed fusible web to muslin scraps. Peel off the paper backing and fuse the muslin scraps over each slit to close.

Use your serger to trim away any excess width on flat bed sheets so they no longer hang below the sides of your comforter. Use the excess fabric as a trim on coordinating throw pillows.

Laura Haynie, Pfaff American Sales Corporation

When purchasing a new comforter, also purchase several matching or coordinating flat sheets. Use the sheets to make pillows, window treatments, and decorative accessories for a truly coordinated room.

June Mellinger, Brother International Corporation

Chapter 5

Just as sewing machines keep changing and improving,

so do sergers. Innovations in serger feet now make it

easier than ever to insert elastic, make belt loops, and

apply lace. The introduction of the cover stitch has

given sewers the ability to incorporate "ready-to-wear"

The Overlock

finishes in their sewing projects. In this chapter, our

sewing experts share their favorite techniques and tips,

from basic to decorative, for easy fuss-free serging.

French Seams

A serged seam is useful for most sewing projects, but there are times when an enclosed seam is a bit more practical. Use French seams for sheers and loosely woven fabrics, or when a more "finished" seam is desired.

1 Place fabric wrong sides together and, using a 3-thread overlock stitch, serge, trimming off ¼″ of the seam allowance.

2 Fold the fabric, right sides together, enclosing the serged seam and press. Using a zipper foot, straight-stitch close to the serged stitching.

Wide Elastic Insertion

Sergers are wonderful for sewing elastic into all types of garments. They can be used to eliminate traditional waistband casings and streamline garment construction.

Wide Elastic Insertion *continued*

1 Cut the elastic to the desired measurement plus 1″. Overlap the ends of the elastic by ½″ and secure with a zigzag stitch. Divide the elastic and garment edge into fourths and mark.

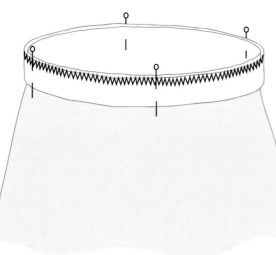

2 Pin the elastic to the wrong side of the garment at the marks, keeping the edge of the elastic even with the raw edge of the garment. Disengage the serger knife and serge the elastic in place, stretching the elastic flat to fit between the pins.

3 Turn the elastic to the inside of the garment. To secure the elastic, "stitch-in-the-ditch" at the side seams and front and back seams through all layers.

4 Stitch several rows of topstitching through all the waistband layers, stretching the elastic in front and behind the foot as you sew. (*Note*: If the elastic has stretched out of shape, it may be steamed back with an iron.)

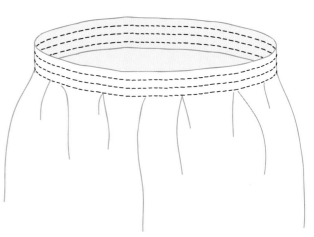

Serger Tassels

Nancy Jewell, Husqvarna Viking®

Finding the just-right tassel to coordinate with a project can sometimes be an impossible task. Husqvarna Viking suggests using your serger to create decorative tassels. Combine thread colors and use decorative threads in various textures to create one-of-a-kind tassels.

1 Set your serger for a rolled edge. Thread the machine with a decorative thread in the upper looper and all-purpose sewing threads in coordinating or contrasting colors in the needle and lower looper.

2 Place a heavy "filler" thread, such as pearl cotton, between the knife and the needle. Serge, forming the rolled edge over the pearl cotton. For each tassel, stitch a serger chain approximately 9 yards long.

3 Cut off 1 yard of the chain and wrap the remaining 8 yards around a 4½″ piece of cardboard. Cut a 12″ piece of chain and insert it through the loops at the upper edge of the cardboard and tie the ends together. Apply seam sealant to the lower edge of the loops. When dry, cut through the loops.

4 Remove the cardboard. Hold the tassel strands together tightly and wrap the top of the tassel with wire about 1″ down from the top. Using a piece of the remaining chain, cover the wire and secure the chain in place with a glue gun.

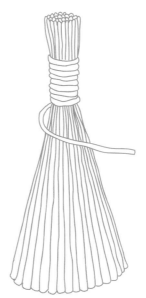

Easy Lacing Guide

Paula Spoon, Elna USA

Add lace edging to hemlines with ease using the cover stitch and one of Elna's lacing guides.

1 Set the serger to a wide cover stitch and attach the chain-stitch foot "F". Position the lace attachment on the needle plate.

2 Turn under ¼" along the edge of your hem. Feed the fabric into the serger through the bottom slot of the lace attachment and feed the lace through the top slot of the attachment. Stitch in place.

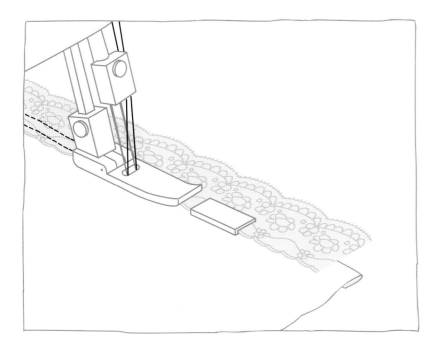

One-Step Belt Loops

Paula Spoon, Elna USA

Use the belt-loop foot to create one-step belt loops like those found in ready-to-wear. Belt loop strips also can be used to create decorative details like cross-hatching and lattice work.

1 Set the serger for a cover stitch and attach the belt-loop foot.

2 Cut a bias strip 1⅛″ wide by 6″ longer than the required length. Feed the bias strip into the front of the foot, pull it through with a stiletto or needle, and place it under the serger needles.

3 Begin sewing. The edges of the bias strip will automatically fold to the underside creating the belt loops. To add bias strips to fabric for decorative purposes, simply place the fabric under the bias strip. The strips will attach to the fabric as they feed through the foot.

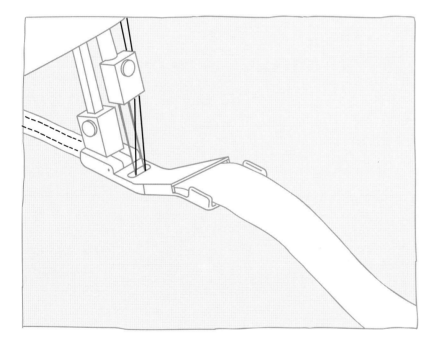

Flatlocking Lace

Sara Meyer, Bernina of America

Use the 2-thread flatlock stitch to stitch two layers of lace or eyelet trim at one time. Use decorative threads to add unexpected detail to the center of the lace.

1 Thread the serger for a 2-thread flatlock stitch with decorative thread in the lower looper.

2 Place a strip of lace on the right side of each fabric piece. With the wrong sides of the fabric together, stitch the seam. *Note*: The lace will be on top and bottom as the fabric feeds through the serger. Open the fabric flat.

Flat Decorative Edges

Keri Morales, Brother International Corporation

Decorative edges that won't lie flat are a thing of the past when using this simple technique from Brother.

1 Set the serger for a 3-thread overlock stitch or rolled hem. Thread the machine with decorative thread of Woolly Nylon™ in the loopers.

2 Place a 3″-wide strip of lightweight stabilizer under the edge of the fabric and stitch through all layers. Gently tear away the stabilizer when the stitching is complete.

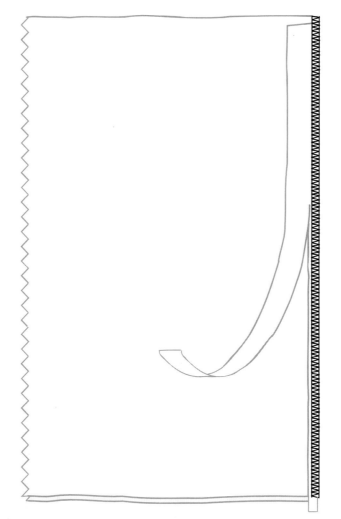

Simple Belt Loops

Kelly Latreille, Baby Lock USA

Create quick-and-easy fabric belt loops using the 2-thread flatlock stitch. This is the fool-proof way to create professional-looking belt loops if your machine is not equipped to do a cover stitch.

1 Set the serger for a 2-thread flatlock stitch and thread will all-purpose thread. Cut a strip of fabric 1½" wide by the required length.

2 Fold the fabric strip, wrong sides together, and stitch along the raw edge. Gently pull the seam flat. Fold the fabric so the seam is centered on one side and press flat.

3 Topstitch the edges of the belt loop using a conventional sewing machine.

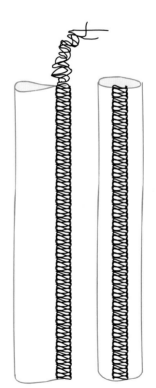

Serger Blanket Stitch

Nina Kay Donovan, Husqvarna Viking®

A decorative blanket-binding stitch is the ideal finishing touch for a polar fleece jacket or flannel pajamas. Topstitching thread and a 2-thread flatlock are all you need to create this unique edge finish.

Serger Blanket Stitch *continued*

1 Set the serger for a 2-thread flatlock stitch, threading the needle with top-stitching thread and the lower looper with serger thread.

2 Place strips of water-soluble stabilizer under the right side of the edge to be serged. Serge along the edge through all the layers.

3 When the stitching is completed, firmly grip the loose edge of the stabilizer and pull it toward the edge of the fabric. Work the stitches around the edge to create a blanket-stitch effect.

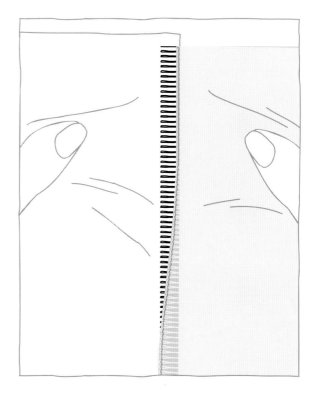

4 Once the stabilizer has been turned completely around the edge, tear it away. Spritz the excess stabilizer with water to dissolve.

Tips from the Experts

If your serger thread is twisting as it comes through the thread guides, turn the spool or cone upside down. Take the coneholder off the spindle, place the cone on the spindle upside down, and put the coneholder down inside the cone to keep it from wobbling. This can eliminate unexplainable "hiccups" that are caused by thread twists as they come through the tension disks.

Laura Haynie, Pfaff American Sales Corporation

Don't be afraid to run your serger at high speeds. Sergers were designed to go fast and perform at their best when running at a high speed. You have better control over your fabric and will serge straighter if you serge faster.

Keri Morales, Brother International Corporation

When was the last time you changed your serger needles? Perhaps it's time to treat your serger to a new set of needles. Although serger needles do not need to be changed as often as needles on a conventional machine, they do need to be changed frequently as they are stitching at a very high speed and tend to dull faster.

Keri Morales, Brother International Corporation

Chapter 6

If you're like me, there are notions that are always at

your fingertips because they are truly useful. Then

there is that notion that you bought and forgot

what it is used for. Years later, you finally have a

Worthy Notions

use for it, but it took you longer to find the gadget

than it would have taken to complete your task with-

out it! Here are 10 notions that I find truly useful and

am glad to have handy on a regular basis.

Top-10 Notions You and I Can't Live Without

#10 — Seams Great®

Rolled hems that roll right off the fabric and leave you with a scarf in one hand and a rolled hem in the other can be frustrating, to say the least. Seams Great is a bias-cut nylon tricot that adds just the right amount of stability to keep rolled edges on the edge where they belong.

#9 — Hump Jumper

Are you still using folded cardboard to stitch over various thickness of fabric? The Hump Jumper is an inexpensive notion that will do the same thing for you. This plastic tool sits behind, next to, or in front of the presser foot to level it when sewing over bulky seams, like heavy, denim fabric hems. Some versatile tools of this nature can be stacked for varying thicknesses.

#8 — Needle Release®

A must, when using the sticky-backed stabilizers as I did for the projects in my embroidery book! This is simply a bag containing a treated felt that dissolves any gummy residue and lubricates the needle. Sew directly through the bag four or five times to remove sticky residue from your needle.

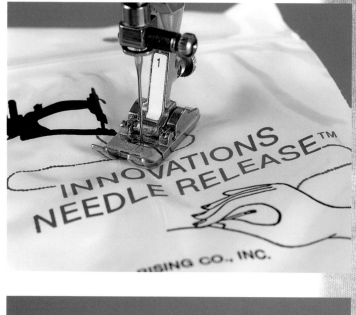

#7 — Yardstick Compass

Although not a necessity for every sewer, I just love this gadget. It has two adjustable holders that attach to a yardstick or ruler. One end is a metal point, the other a lead point, so you can draw exact circles up to 72″ in diameter. It's perfect for home decorating projects like circular tablecloths or round pillows.

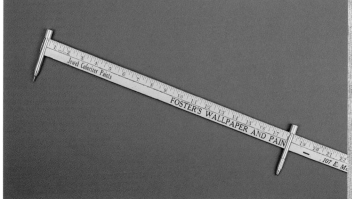

#6 — Bodkin

I think I've been using this tool for about 20 years! It's similar to tweezers with teeth. A small ring slides along the bodkin to securely hold elastic or cord. Insert the curved end of the bodkin into the casing and pull it through. It's great for garments in progress or for reinserting cords that have been accidentally removed.

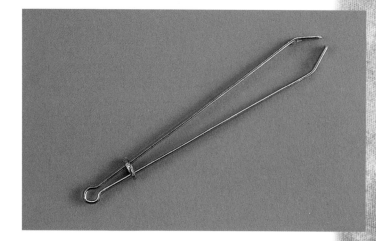

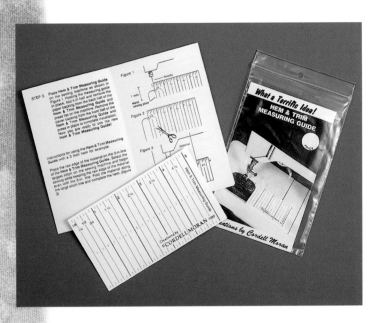

#5 — Hem & Trim Measuring Guide

Until I found this notion, I used everything from adhesive bandages to washable crayons to mark extra-wide seams. This is an adhesive-backed guide that adheres to your sewing machine and measures seams up to 5″ away from the needle. Marked in ⅛″ increments, it's the ideal measuring tool.

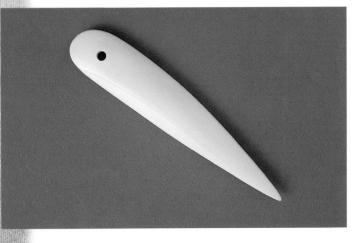

#4 — Point Turner

I must admit I was a holdout for this notion, but after one semi-disastrous point-turning experience using the tip of a scissors . . . I bought a point turner on my next visit to the fabric store! Use the pointed end of the turner to turn sharp points and corners right side out. The curved edge also can be used to hold seams open for pressing or for creasing.

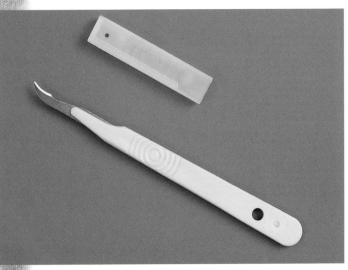

#3 — Serger Seam Ripper

The quickest and easiest way to remove a 3-thread overlock stitch is with this seam ripper. The curved blade slides through serger stitches and protects your fabric from being cut accidentally.

#2 — Fray Check™ or No Fray

I use this notion all the time. It's used to secure serger seams, particularly rolled hems on napkins. Place a drop on the thread tails and trim excess threads away. Seam sealant is also great to carry in your purse—it works wonders on runs in your stockings—and a bit more discreet than colored nail polish!

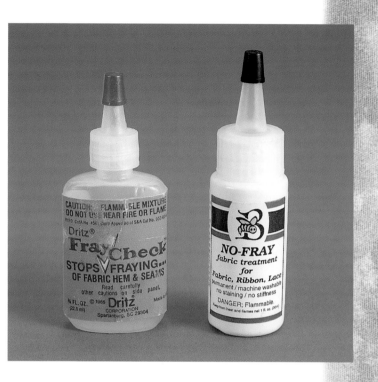

And the number one sewing notion in my sewing room is...

#1 — Buttonhole Cutter

This is my favorite notion—hands down. I actually look forward to making button-holes so I can open them with this tool! The cutter looks like a small chisel and comes with a small wooden block. Simply center the buttonhole on the block and cut through the center with the cutter. Neatly cut buttonholes every time! If you are using a loosely woven fabric put a bit of Fray Check in the center of the buttonhole and let dry before cutting open. (Perhaps this explains why Fray Check™ is favorite notion number 2 !)

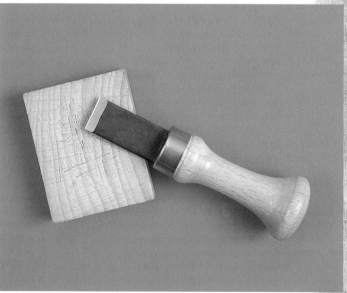

INDEX